Ireland – A Graphic History

Morgan Llywelyn is the author of several highly acclaimed historical novels about Ireland and the Irish people, including the bestselling *Lion of Ireland*, which sold over 15 million copies worldwide and the film version of which is currently being produced by a Hollywood studio. Born in New York City of Celtic origins, she now lives in Ireland.

Michael Scott has written numerous novels based on legends, history and folklore. He is the author of *Irish Folk and Fairytales*, which has sold in excess of 2 million copies.

Eoin Coveney trained under Will Eisner and has worked as a designer and illustrator for many years in both Dublin and Germany. He has also contributed to *2000 AD*.

IRELAND
A Graphic History

Morgan Llywelyn and Michael Scott

Illustrated by Eoin Coveney

with the assistance of
David Smith, Inker
Roger Horgan, Inker
Laurence Herbert, Colourist
Vicky Jocher, Colourist
Damian Foley, Colourist
John Hussey, Colourist

Produced by
National Cartoon Company of Ireland Ltd.

ELEMENT
Shaftesbury, Dorset ● Rockport, Massachusetts
Brisbane, Queensland

Illustrations © The Cartoon Company Ltd. 1995
Text © Morgan Llywelyn and Michael Scott 1995
Published in Great Britain in 1995 by
Element Books Ltd
Shaftesbury, Dorset

Published in the USA in 1995 by
Element, Inc.
42 Broadway, Rockport, MA 01966

Published in Australia in 1995 by
Element Books Ltd
for Jacaranda Wiley Ltd
33 Park Road, Milton, Brisbane, 4064

Originated by Dudley Stewart.
Compiled by Grainne O'Rourke.
Designers and Illustrators provided by Springboard.
Cover illustration by Steve Simpson.
Cover design by National Cartoon Company of Ireland Ltd.
Design by National Cartoon Company of Ireland Ltd.
Typesetting and colour separation by
Dublin Online Typographic Services Ltd.
Printed in Scotland by
Bath Press Colourbooks.

British Library Cataloguing in Publication
data available

Library of Congress Cataloguing in Publication
data available

ISBN 1–85230–627–0

FOREWORD

In some mysterious way a nation sometimes becomes cloaked in a particular image which is then enshrined as its persona.

People have long perceived Ireland to be a romantic, mystical isle, a quiet place out of time. The Irish were portrayed as an engaging race, singers of songs and tellers of tales, equally fond of a fight or a frolic. Talking about Erin summoned visions of shamrocks, thatched cottages, and leprechauns, a quaint, charming, fairytale land.

So it is hardly surprising that those of us abroad were dumbstruck by news of bombings, terrorism and murder splashing Ireland's legendary green fields with blood. We simply did not understand.

To our questions, the response was, "Oh, the Troubles! It's an ancient struggle that will never be resolved. Ireland is haunted by her history etc., etc." One got bar-stool explanations in simple black and white. This side was good, that side was evil. But the images flickering nightly on the television screen defied such simplistic analysis.

"Why is this happening?" we wondered.

The answers surely lie in the history of the island. In order to understand, Ireland's past must be seen as a whole, on a broad canvas.

Such a view is the intention of this book. Because the saga is told in a graphic idiom we are able to "see" to visualise it. The writers and artists who have undertaken this ambitious endeavour have employed the graphic narrative form of storytelling. This sophisticated compound of words and sequentially arranged images, this new literacy, is eminently suited to the task.

IRELAND A GRAPHIC HISTORY is a book to read and re-read, and refer to as future history is made.

WILL EISNER
FLORIDA

To the memory of Eilis Dillon

Who has fully realised that history is not contained
in thick books but lives in our very blood?

Carl Jung (1875 - 1961)

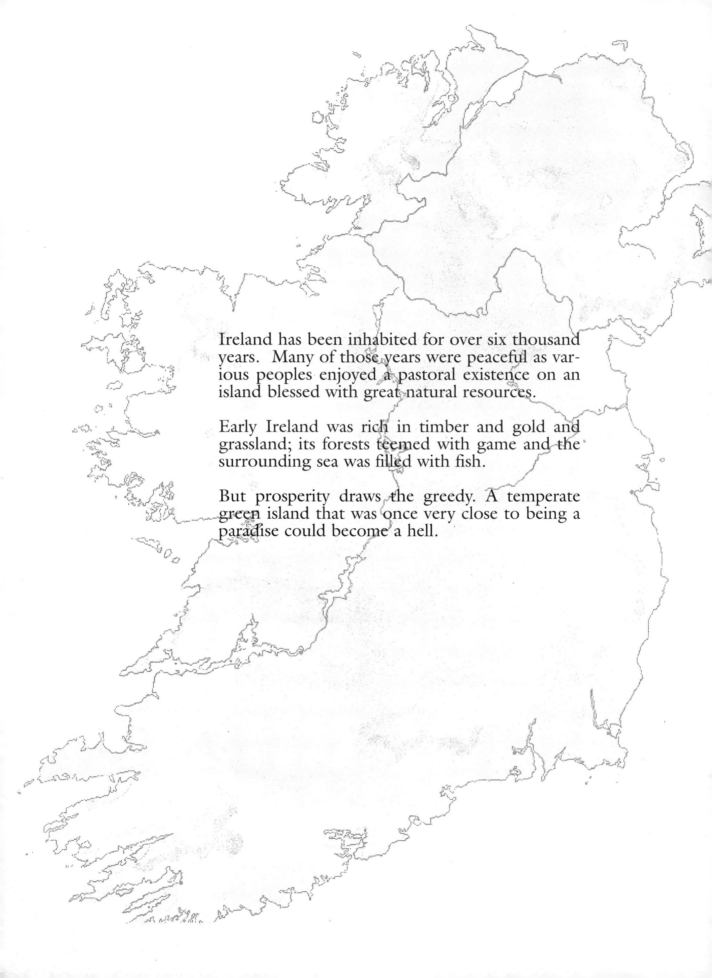

Ireland has been inhabited for over six thousand years. Many of those years were peaceful as various peoples enjoyed a pastoral existence on an island blessed with great natural resources.

Early Ireland was rich in timber and gold and grassland; its forests teemed with game and the surrounding sea was filled with fish.

But prosperity draws the greedy. A temperate green island that was once very close to being a paradise could become a hell.

PROLOGUE

INTRODUCTION

The present-day city of Belfast stands at the head of Belfast Lough, shouldered by mountains and traversed by the Lagan river. A city could hope for no lovelier site. Inhabited since earliest times, Belfast – from the Irish Beal Feirste, meaning the Ford of the Sandbank – has been the site of Stone Age and Bronze Age settlements and there are still remnants of Iron Age hillforts not far from the city centre.

Belfast's modern history began with Baron Arthur Chichester, who built a castle there in 1611 and gained a charter of incorporation from the English crown in 1613. The town continued to flourish as various industries were developed. The majority of the population were Protestant English and Scottish colonists, but a significant Catholic minority formed a large part of the labour force. A busy port and shipbuilding centre, by the end of the 17th century Belfast became one of the world's foremost linen centres as French Huguenots refugees settled there, bringing with them their skills in weaving and clothmaking.

In the twentieth century the name of Belfast was heard round the world when the famous Titanic was built in her shipyards. But as if a harbinger of tragedy to come, the Titanic sank shortly before World War I. Then followed Partition, with much of Ulster remaining part of the United Kingdom while the rest of Ireland gained independence. Belfast was severely damaged by air raids during World War II. The city was rebuilt, only to be torn by dissension following a Roman Catholic civil rights campaign in 1968. Street riots and escalating violence soon followed. When British troops arrived to deal with the disorders, an increased use of bombs and firearms by both sides turned the lovely city on the Lagan into a battleground.

Belfast today is the capital of Northern Ireland, which comprises six counties of ancient Ulster. The city boasts such educational centres as Queen's University, the Presbyterian College and the Royal Belfast Academic Institution. Its streets, like most Irish streets, are thronged with young people. But beneath the beauty of the setting and the faces of youth ... lie the scars of ancient wars.

BELFAST, SPRING 1994.

FROM THE DISTANCE IT LOOKS LIKE ANY OTHER CITY, TALL, HANDSOME BUILDINGS, TOWER BLOCKS, SHOPPING CENTRES, WIDE OPEN GREENS...

... BUT THIS IS BELFAST, IRELAND.

SOLDIERS, AND ARMED POLICE PATROL THE STREETS...

... KEEPING THE PEACE.

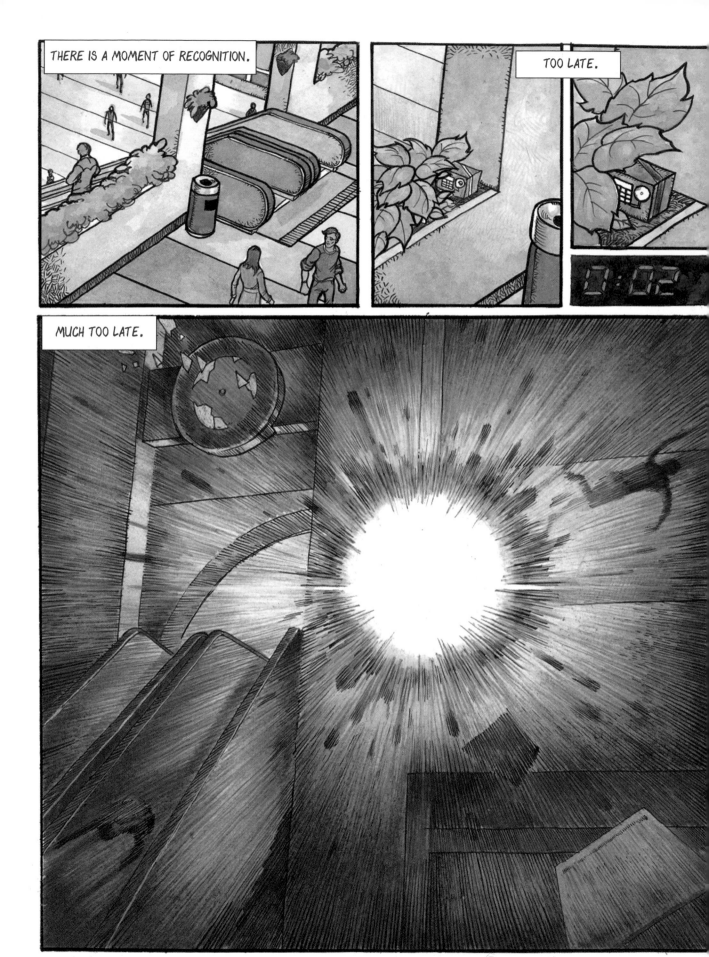

WHEN THE SMOKE CLEARS, ONLY BODIES REMAIN.

SOME ARE ALREADY DEAD...

...OTHERS DYING.

A DESPERATE FIGHT FOR LIFE BEGINS.

A GENERATION OF SURGEONS HAVE HONED THEIR SKILLS ON INJURIES LIKE THESE ...

A GENERATION OF FAMILIES HAVE WAITED IN ROOMS LIKE THESE...

WHEN ALL ELSE HAS FAILED, ONLY PRAYERS REMAIN.

AND SOME PRAYERS CALL OLDER GODS.

CHAPTER ONE

THE MYSTERY OF NEWGRANGE

INTRODUCTION

The first known settlers in Ireland were Mesolithic, or Stone Age people, who arrived in small boats from the European continent.

Fishermen and hunter-gatherers, they settled around the mouths of rivers. In time they learned to plant grain and other crops and developed complex rituals to guarantee the fertility of the land.

These were not grunting cavemen, but members of a highly organised and intelligent society. They studied the earth and the sky and attempted to manipulate their environment in ways we do not yet fully understand.

As other Neolithic people would do centuries later at Stonehenge and Avebury, they built temples of stone incorporating the astronomy of their age, accurate calendars of the solstices, the equinoxes, and other phenomena.

Their foremost ritual centre was at Newgrange, on the River Boyne. A large area of the Boyne Valley was deliberately turned into a ritual landscape.

This sacred precinct stretched as far as the Hill of Tara to the south and the Hill of Tailte to the west, but the most spectacular development took place in a great bend of the river to the east, an easy journey by boat to the rivermouth and the Irish Sea beyond.

Here three immense earthwork mounds were erected over carefully designed and beautifully decorated stone chambers and passages.

It may truthfully be said that these are the oldest engineered buildings on the planet, predating the Great Pyramids. They were surrounded by a number of smaller tumuli, the overall arrangement reflecting their builders' view of sacred patterns perceived in nature.

Here the first Irish men and women worshipped the Great Fire in the Sky as the principle of Life and welcomed its warming rays into the womb of the Earth at sunrise on the winter solstice.

WINTER SOLSTICE... 5,000 YEARS AGO.

THE PEOPLE GATHER.

EOLANG, A PRIEST OF THE PEOPLE.

TO AWAIT THE DAWN.

BUT ONLY THE PRIESTS ENTER THE MOUND.

SUNRISE.

THE SHAFT OF LIGHT REACHES INTO THE HEART OF THE MOUND.

THE CEREMONY IS COMPLETE, THE SUN HAS RETURNED. THE EARTH AND THE PEOPLE WILL BE MADE FERTILE AGAIN.

BUT FOR EOLANG AND BRIGENTA, HIS MATE...

...THE GODS HAVE ALREADY GIVEN THEIR BLESSING.

LIFE COULD BE SHORT...

...AND BRUTAL.

THE OUTCOME WAS INEVITABLE...

DEATH...

...OR SLAVERY.

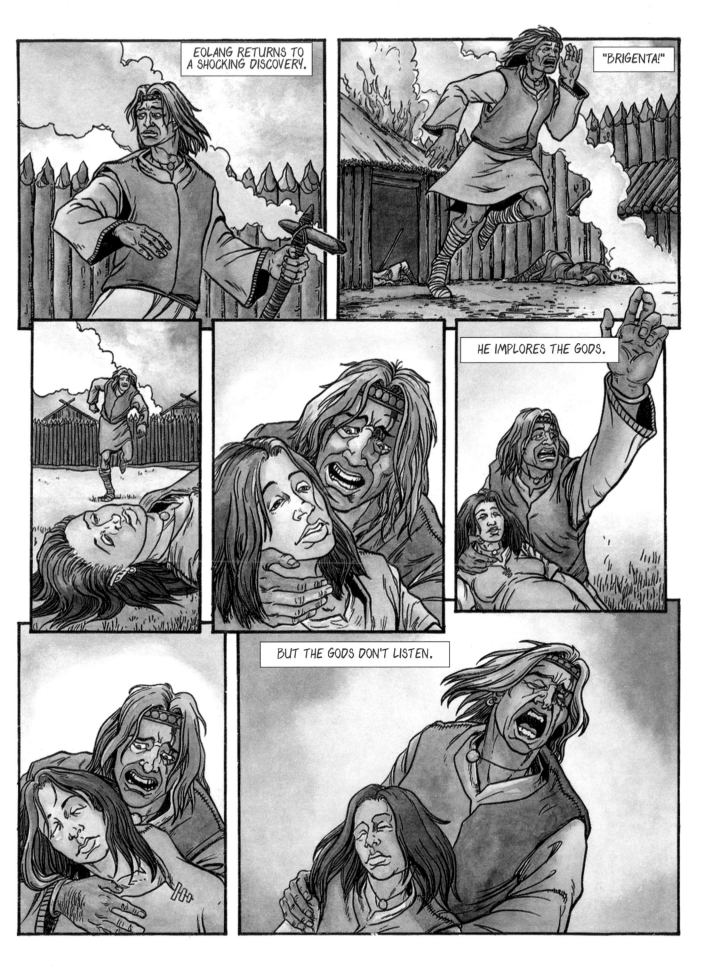

"HELP ME. USE THE POWER IN THE MOUND. BRING LIFE BACK TO BRIGENTA".

"I WILL NOT WASTE IT."

AND SO EOLANG COMMITS THE ULTIMATE SACRILEGE.

THE HEAD PRIEST REFUSES.

"I CANNOT".

"CANNOT OR **WILL NOT.**"

AND FOR HIS CRIME HE IS BANISHED FROM THE PRIESTHOOD AND THE SAFETY OF THE VILLAGE... A DEATH SENTENCE.

BUT EOLANG DOES NOT DIE. HIS FATE FESTERS WITHIN HIM.

AND IN THE SEASONS THAT FOLLOW, HE RAILS AGAINST THE PRIESTS.

"THESE ARE OUR GODS... NOT THE PRIESTS."

"HERESY!"

"OUR FOREFATHERS BUILT THIS MOUND...

"... WITH STONE AND SWEAT AND BLOOD. IT IS OURS."

"THE LAND WAS LAID BARE."

"HOW MANY GAVE UP THEIR LIVES TO BUILD THIS PLACE?"

"AND NOW IT HAS BEEN TAKEN FROM US. BY THEM!"

"THE HERETIC HAS RETURNED."

"STONE HIM..."

"...KILL HIM."

"NO."

"LET HIM SPEAK."

"YOU HAVE THE COURAGE TO SPEAK THE WORDS WE HAVE ALL FELT FOR A LONG TIME. BUT THE PRIESTS..."

"...THEIR TIME IS OVER. THEY WERE ONCE OUR SERVANTS... NOW THEY ARE OUR MASTERS."

"OUR FOREFATHERS WORSHIPPED STRONG GODS, WORTHY GODS A MAN WOULD BE PROUD TO WORSHIP."

THE PRIESTS RETURN.

"HIS WORDS WILL ANGER THE GODS, BRING RUIN ON US."

"THIS PLACE IS THE SYMBOL OF PRIEST'S POWER. WE MUST DESTROY IT..."

THE HOLY PLACE WAS DESTROYED BUT EOLANG FELT NO SATISFACTION. IT WOULD NOT BRING HIS BELOVED BACK.

"ARE YOU SATISFIED NOW?"

"DO YOU KNOW WHAT YOU HAVE DONE? BY DESTROYING THIS PLACE, THE SACRED HEART OF THE ISLAND YOU HAVE DOOMED THIS LAND NEVER TO KNOW PEACE."

"I CURSE YOU NOW, AYE, AND YOUR BELOVED..."

"...TO WALK THIS LAND TO LIVE, TIME AND TIME AGAIN UNTIL THE LAND IS AT PEACE."

"IT WILL TAKE AN ETERNITY."

CHAPTER TWO

THE FIRE ON THE HILL:
ST. PATRICK

INTRODUCTION

Patrick was not Irish at all, but was born somewhere on the island of Britain. He was of the Celtic race, however. After the Neolithic inhabitants died out a succession of Celtic tribes from mainland Europe had settled throughout the British Isles, bringing with them first the Bronze Age and then the Age of Iron. Later all fell under the sway of Roman civilisation – except Ireland, which Caesar never attempted to conquer.

Nor was Patrick the first Christian missionary to visit pagan Ireland. His father Calpurnius was a British civil servant serving under Roman government in the fifth century A.D. The Christianised Romans had by then converted many Britons, and the Church was interested in converting pagans even in such remote lands as Ireland. Several missionaries had been sent to that island before a boy called Patricius was captured by Irish pirates and sold as a slave when he was sixteen years old.

He became a shepherd in the west of Ireland. At that time the island was ruled by a famous king called Niall of the Nine Hostages, whose descendants would claim the Hill of Tara as their royal seat. The lonely life of a shepherd gave young Patricius – or Patrick as the Irish called him – much time for thought and contemplation. He began to have visions. Obeying these visions, after six years he escaped from Ireland and eventually found his way home again, then went on to take instruction in the Church. After many years he became a bishop.

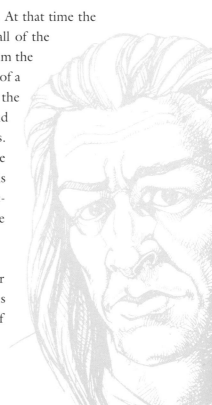

But he was not through with Ireland, nor Ireland with him. His visionary dreams returned, urging him to go back to the land of his captivity and convert the pagans there.

IRELAND 432 AD.
A SPARK IN THE DARKNESS.

PATRICK THE MISSIONARY.

THE BANQUETING HALL AT TARA.

KING LAOGHAIRE
AND QUEEN ANGRAS.

A DRUID APPROACHES.

"BLASPHEMY."

KING LAOGHAIRE CALLS
HIS CHIEFTAINS TOGETHER.

THEY RIDE OUT IN SEARCH OF THE FIRE ON SLANE.

KING LAOGHAIRE CONFRONTS PATRICK.

"MY DRUIDS TELL ME THAT NO FIRE CAN BURN BEFORE THE DRUID FIRE ON TARA HAS BROUGHT LIFE BACK TO THE LAND."

"I DO NOT ACCEPT YOUR PAGAN BELIEFS."

"THEN YOU WILL DIE."

"MY GOD WILL PROTECT ME."

"BRING HIM TO TARA. HAVE HIM EXPLAIN HIS GOD."

"ONCE WE HAVE HIM IN TARA, KILL HIM!"

AN ELDERLY CHIEFTAIN STEPS OUT FROM BEHIND THE KING.

"I KNOW YOU. YOU ARE THE ESCAPED SLAVE, PATRICIUS."

"YES, I AM. I WAS ONCE A SLAVE IN THIS COUNTRY."

"I WAS A BOY OF SIXTEEN WHEN I WAS KIDNAPPED BY NIALL OF THE NINE HOSTAGES, LAOGHAIRE'S FATHER."

"I WAS TAKEN ACROSS THE SEA TO IRELAND."

"THEN SOLD INTO SLAVERY AND TAKEN TO THE FAR WEST."

"I SPENT SIX YEARS AS A SLAVE ON THE MOUNTAINSIDE."

"AND DURING THAT TIME, GOD SPOKE TO ME."

"WHEN I WAS 22, GOD URGED ME TO FLEE IRELAND."

"I FOUND A SHIP."

"RELUCTANTLY, THEY TOOK ME ON BOARD, AND I EVENTUALLY RETURNED HOME."

"I KNEW GOD WANTED ME TO BE A PRIEST, SO I WENT TO GAUL, WHERE I TRAINED."

"BUT I NEVER FORGOT IRELAND."

"AND WHEN I BECAME A BISHOP I FELT GOD CALLING ME BACK TO ERIN. IT WAS A CALL I COULD NOT RESIST."

THE COURT IS DIVIDED BY PATRICK'S ELOQUENCE, SOME ELECTING TO FOLLOW PATRICK, OTHERS CLINGING TO THE OLD WAYS.

"TO REMAIN KING, I MUST KEEP TO THE FAITH OF MY FATHERS."

"HAVE ANY OF OUR GODS EVER DIED FOR US? NO, THEY DEMAND SACRIFICE."

"IT HAS BEEN A LONG TIME..."

"YOU SHOULD NEVER HAVE GONE AWAY."

"I WAITED FOR YOU."

"I WAITED A LONG TIME."

"WHY ARE YOU HERE?"

"I AM THE QUEEN'S MAID. AND YOU – WHAT ARE YOU DOING HERE?"

"I FOLLOW PATRICK."

"I ALWAYS SAID I WOULD COME BACK FOR YOU. MARRY ME."

"I CANNOT. I AM BETROTHED TO ANOTHER."

"MARRY ME. TODAY IS A SPECIAL DAY FOR THE CHRISTIANS, EASTER SUNDAY."

"TODAY IS BELTANE, SACRED TO MY PEOPLE – YOUR PEOPLE. I WILL MARRY YOU ON ONE CONDITION: RENOUNCE THIS NEW RELIGION."

"I CANNOT."

THE FEAST OF BELTANE ... AND A WEDDING FEAST.

CHAPTER THREE
VIKING

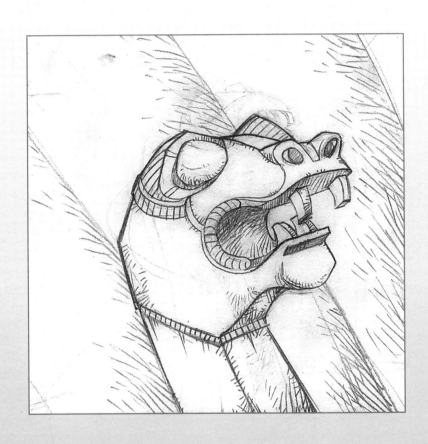

INTRODUCTION

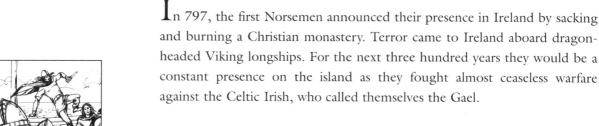

In 797, the first Norsemen announced their presence in Ireland by sacking and burning a Christian monastery. Terror came to Ireland aboard dragon-headed Viking longships. For the next three hundred years they would be a constant presence on the island as they fought almost ceaseless warfare against the Celtic Irish, who called themselves the Gael.

The Norsemen were soon followed by the Danes, and the two Scandinavian peoples not only fought the Gael, but sometimes each other. They came from lands with long cold winters, hard lands that bred strong men who took to the sea out of necessity. Scandinavian farming provided the bare necessities of life, but the northlands had few luxuries.

Ireland, on the other hand, had abundant natural resources – gold, timber, cattle, fish, and beautiful children that brought high prices in the Mediterranean slave markets. These, combined with its lush and temperate climate, made Ireland seem a paradise to the sea rovers from the north.

For the Vikings were not merely plunderers, but traders engaged in building a vast commercial network. They sailed as far as the Baltic, Russia, and Byzantium, and soon learned the value of Irish craftsmanship abroad. Irish churches, like Irish chieftains, were laden with ornaments of gold and silver set with precious gems, and commanded high prices throughout the known world. The Irish were literate, which the Vikings were not, and even housed their books in jewel-encrusted caskets.

So much wealth, combined with a moderate climate and excellent harbours, was irresistible. The Vikings built cities such as Dublin, Waterford, Wexford, and Limerick to serve as trading ports. They introduced urban commerce into what had been a totally pastoral way of life. As the years passed Scandinavian men also sent for women from home, or married Irish women and raised families on the green island.

The Vikings had come to stay.

A RING FORT ON THE EAST COAST OF IRELAND.

"VIKINGS."

"THE VIKINGS ARE COMING!"

TERROR GRIPS THE VILLAGE.

SEPARATED FROM HER MOTHER, ONE GIRL RETURNS TO THE SHELTER OF HER HOME.

THE PAGAN RAIDERS SWARM ASHORE.

FEW CAN STAND AGAINST THE VIKING WARRIORS.

THE WOMEN ATTEMPT TO SAVE THEIR CHILDREN.

"MY DAUGHTER? HAVE YOU SEEN MY DAUGHTER?"

NO ONE HAS.

"LEAVE HER. THERE'S NOTHING YOU CAN DO FOR HER NOW."

THE VIKINGS TAKE NO PRISONERS EXCEPT THE YOUNG, AS SLAVES.

THE CHIEFTAIN'S SON HAD NOT IMAGINED HE WOULD FEEL SUCH FEAR...

... HIS FATHER HAD ALWAYS TOLD HIM THAT KILLING WAS EASY.

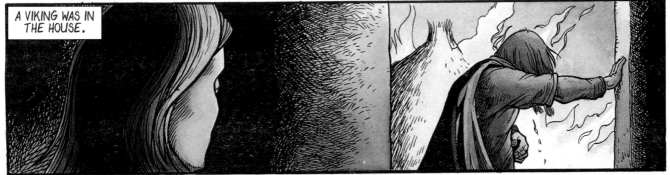

A VIKING WAS IN THE HOUSE.

THIS WAS NO VIKING. THIS WAS A BOY ...

... THE SAME AGE AS HER BROTHER.

"A PRISONER. A FINE CATCH. TRULY YOU ARE MY SON."

SHE HAD BEEN MISTAKEN. HE WAS A VIKING.

WATCHING HER GO, HE FELT ...

... GUILTY.

SLAVES BOUND FOR THE SLAVE PENS OF DUBLIN.

"MY DAUGHTER, GIVE ME BACK MY DAUGHTER!"

THE SECOND KILLING WAS EVEN EASIER.

MOTHER.

THE VIKINGS SET SAIL WITH THEIR PLUNDER.

"YOU DID WELL TODAY, MY SON. I AM PROUD OF YOU."

"WHY DO WE DO THIS?"

"BECAUSE IT IS THE WAY OF THE WORLD. COMPARE OUR HOMELAND TO THIS PLACE ... WHERE THE SOIL IS RICH, THE CATTLE CAN GROW FAT ... AND THERE IS GOLD APLENTY. WE ARE WARRIORS, CONQUERORS... WHAT WE WANT WE TAKE."

"THE CHOICE OF THE SPOILS IS YOURS. TAKE WHAT YOU WANT."

"GIVE ME THE GIRL."

"AS YOU WISH ..."

" ... IT IS A GOOD CHOICE. SHE WILL FETCH A FINE PRICE."

SHE LUNGES FOR HIM.

"VIXEN!"

"NO! SHE IS MY PROPERTY NOW."

THE TRADE IN SLAVES MADE FORTUNES FOR MANY MEN.

"A GOOD CROP TODAY. FINE. STRONG."

"LET ME MAKE YOU AN OFFER FOR THAT ONE."

"SHE IS NOT FOR SALE."

THERE ARE THINGS HE MUST SAY TO THIS GIRL, EXPLANATIONS HE MUST MAKE... HE TRIES TO TALK TO HER.

BUT THEY HAVE NO COMMON LANGUAGE.

IF ONLY HE COULD MAKE HER UNDERSTAND.

SHE HAS TO KNOW THAT HE MEANS HER NO HARM...

WHAT WAS HE TRYING TO TELL HER.

WAS HE TRYING TO TELL HER SHE WOULD SPEND THE REST OF HER LIFE AS A SLAVE?

"I WILL TAKE CARE OF YOU. I WILL LOOK AFTER YOU."

"WHERE HAS THAT BOY GONE?"

WITHOUT WORDS, HE TRIES TO COMMUNICATE BY TOUCH. A GIFT TO PLEASE HER.

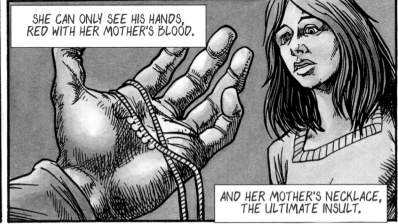

SHE CAN ONLY SEE HIS HANDS, RED WITH HER MOTHER'S BLOOD.

AND HER MOTHER'S NECKLACE, THE ULTIMATE INSULT.

"VIKING VERMIN!"

"MY SON!"

A VIKING FUNERAL.

THE GIRL WAS NEVER CAUGHT, THOUGH A HUGE REWARD WAS OFFERED FOR HER.

CHAPTER FOUR
BRIAN BORU

INTRODUCTION

In the tenth century an obscure Irish chieftain from the banks of the Shannon made his reputation fighting Vikings, then rose to become king of the province of Munster and ultimately High King. In the Book of Armagh, Brian Boru would one day style himself Emperor of the Irish.

Ireland had never seen anything like him. He was an exceptional combination of warrior and statesman, a pragmatic strategist who studied the careers of Caesar and Charlemagne, and won as many battles through psychology as with the sword. He also loved poetry and played the harp. During the course of his long life he had several wives and more than thirty concubines, and marriages which he arranged for his children passed his blood into the royal houses of Europe.

Brian Boru was the first to envision an Ireland in which the various peoples would flow together like many streams to form one river. With subtle diplomacy he made allies among the Vikings who had been his enemies and encouraged them to become part of Irish society. During his reign as High King the island enjoyed an era of relative peace and prosperity. He even planned the establishment of a royal dynasty that would carry his vision for Ireland into the future.

Then in 1014, rebellion. Brian had set aside his troublesome wife Gormlaith, a princess of Leinster. By an earlier marriage to a Viking she was mother to Sitric Silkbeard, Viking king of Dublin. Gormlaith and her brother Maelmora encouraged Sitric to call allies from throughout Scandinavia to overthrow Brian and complete the conquest of Ireland. Sitric actually offered his mother in marriage to any northman who killed Brian Boru.

A giant of a man in his seventy third year, Brian Boru rode to battle for the last time. At the fishing weir of Clontarf, north of Dublin, his Irish and Viking allies fought the rebellious Leinstermen and an invasion force of their Viking allies. At the end of that fateful Good Friday Brian had won, and the threat of foreign domination was destroyed ... but at a terrible cost.

TOMAR'S WOOD CLONTARF,
APRIL 23, 1014.

BRODIR, PRINCE OF
MANN.

THE TENT OF BRIAN BORU.

LAITEN THE HERALD APPROACHES.

BRIAN BORU, THE EMPEROR OF THE IRISH

"NEWS OF THE BATTLE."

"THE VIKINGS ARE FLEEING. WE HAVE WON!"

"AND MY SON? WHAT OF MURROUGH?"

"HIS STANDARD HAS FALLEN."

"LEAVE NOW... WE'RE WINNING, GO CLAIM YOUR SHARE OF THE SPOILS."

"YOU WILL BE ALONE."

"WHAT CAN HARM ME NOW?"

IN HIS LONG LIFE HE HAD SEEN SO MUCH DEATH, BUT SURELY TO BURY A SON WAS THE HARDEST TO BEAR.

"THE GODS HAVE LED ME HERE TO THE TENT OF BRIAN BORU."

"YOU HAVE LOST. THE WAR BETWEEN YOUR PEOPLE AND MINE IS OVER."

"NOT YET!"

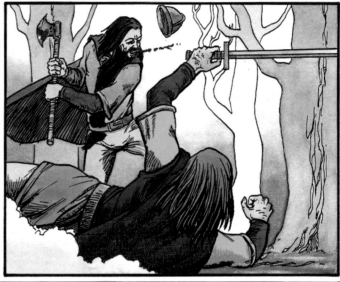

THE BATTLEFIELD STRETCHED FROM FINGAL TO HOWTH. THE RIVER TOLKA RAN RED WITH BLOOD.

IN PLACES THE BATTLE HAD BEEN SO FIERCE THAT THE TREES HAD DRIPPED WITH BLOOD...

AND WHEN THE WARRIORS HAD MOVED ON, THE WOMEN APPEARED SEEKING LOVED ONES, STEALING FROM THE CORPSES, DISPATCHING THE ENEMY WOUNDED.

THE COST HAD BEEN TERRIBLE...

TERRIBLE INDEED.

THE WOUNDED VIKING GROANS.

"DO I KNOW YOU?"

"NO."

"WHAT HAVE YOU DONE?"

"KILLED A MAN."

"MORE THAN A MAN. MUCH MORE."

CHAPTER FIVE

A WEDDING IN WATERFORD: STRONGBOW AND AOIFE

INTRODUCTION

In 1166 Dermot Mac Murrough, king of the Irish province of Leinster, having kidnapped the wife of another king, was stripped of his title and exiled by the High King of Ireland. Dermot sailed to England to apply to Henry II for aid. Eventually he was allowed to recruit an army from among the feudal Norman barons who defended the English borders.

In 1170 a Norman named Richard De Clare brought an army to Ireland to help Dermot regain the kingship of Leinster. De Clare, better known to history as Strongbow, had received a number of promises from the wily Dermot. He had been promised lands which were no longer in Dermot's possession to bestow; he had been promised a kingship that, under Irish law, he could never claim; and he had been promised Dermot's daughter Aoife – Red Eva – in marriage. But Strongbow was unaware that Irish women were free under the law, not property like Norman women. An Irish woman could refuse to marry any man who did not please her.

The arrival of Strongbow and his Norman knights marked the beginning of eight hundred years of conflict between Ireland and England, as the larger island tried again and again to dominate the smaller one. But Strongbow and his men were not thinking in terms of national conquest. Adventurers and mercenaries, they simply wanted land: rich, unspoiled land and a fresh start in a new place. Strongbow himself, a man of Dermot's age, had been stripped of an earldom by Henry II and was as eager as the former king of Leinster to regain status and power. The promises made to him by Dermot seemed to offer one last chance.

The Normans came ashore in the south of Ireland and soon made their way to Waterford, which they put to the sword. During the seven years that remained of his life, Strongbow would win some battles and lose others, though he never got the kingship Dermot had promised him, and Henry II would strip him of most of the lands he claimed.

But as for Aoife ...

ON 25TH AUGUST 1170, RICHARD DE CLARE, KNOWN AS STRONGBOW, CAME TO IRELAND.

HE BROUGHT A LARGE FORCE OF MEN AND HORSES.

"LE GROS IS COMING. HE WILL BE HERE WITHIN THE DAY."

"FIRST WE WILL TAKE WATERFORD, THEN WE WILL TAKE DUBLIN."

"DO YOU TRUST THIS IRISH KING?"

"I'LL KEEP MY WORD. HE HAD BETTER KEEP HIS. HE HAS PROMISED ME LAND, A KINGSHIP AND A WIFE. I WILL HAVE ALL THREE."

"GO TO MACMURROUGH, TELL HIM I AM COMING. AND I WILL EXPECT HIM TO MAKE GOOD HIS PROMISE."

FERNS, DERMOT MACMURROUGH'S FORT.

STRONGBOW'S MESSENGER APPROACHES.

AOIFE OVERHEARS PART OF THE MESSAGE.

"...EXPECTS YOU TO KEEP YOUR PROMISES."

SHE IS UNAWARE OF HER FATHER'S PROMISE.

"STRONGBOW HAS ARRIVED."

MEANWHILE, THE NORMANS ARE FIGHTING THEIR WAY NORTHWARD.

RICHARD DE CLARE'S SKILL WITH THE WELSH LONGBOW GAVE HIM HIS NAME: STRONGBOW.

WATERFORD: 1170.

THE ELECTED CHIEFTAINS OF WATERFORD GO OUT TO FACE THE ADVANCE COMPANY OF THE INVADERS.

THE ADVANCE COMPANY IS UNDER THE COMMAND OF RAYMOND LE GROS.

"STRONGBOW WILL BE
HERE BY EVENING."

"WE HAVE COME TO ASK YOU
TO SPARE OUR CITY."

"KILL THEM!"

THESE NORMAN KNIGHTS HAD LOST EVERYTHING IN ENGLAND. NOW THEY HAD A CHANCE TO CARVE OUT A NEW KINGDOM ON A RICH AND UNSPOILED ISLAND. AS THEY MARCHED ACROSS THE LUSH LANDSCAPE, IT MUST HAVE SEEMED LIKE PARADISE. WORTH FIGHTING FOR ... WORTH DYING FOR.

THE FIRST ATTACK ON THE CITY WAS REPULSED.

LE GROS SPOTS A WOODEN WATCH TOWER.

THE HUT IS ATTACHED TO THE CITY WALLS.

"PULL!"

THE WALLS ARE BREACHED.

THERE WAS BLOODY HAND TO HAND COMBAT IN THE STREETS.

DERMOT AND AOIFE APPROACH THE CITY.

"WHY HAVE YOU BROUGHT ME HERE?"

DERMOT DOES NOT WANT TO ANSWER

"WHY...?"

THE AIR IS THICK WITH SMOKE AND ASH, COATING EVERYTHING IN FILTHY GRIME.

"I NEED YOUR HELP!"

"MINE."

"I HAVE PROMISED YOU TO STRONGBOW!"

"I NEED HIM TO REGAIN MY KINGDOM ..."

"...AND I CANNOT DO IT WITHOUT YOU. HE WANTS A WIFE."

"I AM NO SLAVE TO BE GIVEN AWAY. I AM A FREE WOMAN."

"STRONGBOW IS WAITING."

STRONGBOW STANDS WAITING ON THE STEPS OF THE CHURCH, WAITING FOR HIS PROMISED BRIDE. HE IS UNAWARE THAT SHE HAS THE RIGHT, UNDER IRISH LAW TO REFUSE HIM. NORMAN WOMEN WERE PROPERTY; IRISH WOMEN WERE FREE.

STRONGBOW HAS BEEN PROMISED A PRINCESS...

... HE IS LOOKING AT A SLATTERN.

"WHO IS THIS?"

"MY DAUGHTER AOIFE."

"I AM THE PRINCESS AOIFE."

"SO YOU ARE."

AND IN THAT MOMENT, A GREAT IRISH LOVE STORY BEGAN.

RICHARD DE CLARE MARRIED AOIFE NI MURROUGH ON THE 28TH OF AUGUST, 1170 IN WATERFORD. THERE WERE THIRTY YEARS AND TWO TOTALLY OPPOSED CULTURES BETWEEN THEM. AGAINST ALL THE ODDS, THE MARRIAGE WAS A SUCCESS. THEY REMAINED DEVOTED TO EACH OTHER FOR THE REST OF THEIR LIVES. THUS WERE ENGLAND AND IRELAND JOINED.

CHAPTER SIX
THE LONG MARCH

INTRODUCTION

After Strongbow gained a foothold King Henry II of England claimed Ireland, a claim upheld by the only English-born Pope. A wave of Anglo-Norman knights descended on the island, seeking adventure and land. With them came armour, cavalry, gunpowder. The struggle for the domination of Ireland had begun in earnest and would continue for eight centuries.

The invaders eventually acquired huge landholdings under a Tudor policy known as Surrender and Regrant. If the Irish chieftains who held the land in trust for their tribes were willing to submit to the English crown, the lands were then 'regranted' to them – but only in part – together with English titles. The best of the land was of course withheld, and bestowed on English colonists.

Gaelic Ireland fought back.

By the Elizabethan era the outcome was still uncertain. Many of the Anglo-Normans had become highly Gaelicised; many of the Irish had become Anglicised in an effort to survive. For a time the two cultures strove to blend into one. In the far Southwest, an Irish chieftain called O'Sullivan won the right to style himself Prince of Beare and Bantry by arguing his case in English before an English magistrate.

Then the ambitious Elizabeth I undertook to complete the subjugation of Ireland once and for all. A fresh wave of rebellion swept the land. Led by an Ulster prince, Hugh O'Neill, Gaelic Ireland tried to shake off the tightening chains. Donal O'Sullivan was among those who cast off his fealty to England and wholeheartedly joined with O'Neill.

The Battle of Kinsale in 1602 proved to be decisive. Spanish support promised to the Irish failed to materialise, and Elizabeth's forces were victorious. Following Kinsale, Hugh O'Neill returned to the north and formally offered his submission to representatives of the English queen – without being told that she had just died. Donal O'Sullivan was left in the south, in command of 'the army of Munster'. But he was massively outnumbered, and the English general Carew set about laying waste to Munster to keep O'Sullivan from getting enough supplies to support his army. Other Irish chieftains were bribed to turn against him.

Before dawn on a bitterly cold January morning Donal O'Sullivan Beare and a thousand of his followers – young and old; men, women, and children – set out from Bantry Bay to Leitrim to seek help. O'Sullivan still believed the cause could be won if allies could be rallied, but during the heartbreaking fortnight that followed, all hope died ... as did Gaelic Ireland.

DECEMBER 30TH 1602

DONAL CAM O'SULLIVAN BEARE.

IN O'SULLIVANS RAGGED ARMY, THERE WERE FOUR HUNDRED SOLDIERS.

SIX HUNDRED CIVILIANS.

THE REFUGEES INCLUDED THE CAMP FOLLOWERS, WIVES, SISTERS, AND SWEETHEARTS OF THE SOLDIERS, WHO TENDED THE SICK AND COOKED FOR THEIR MEN.

O'SULLIVAN WAS FIRST ATTACKED TWO DAYS LATER.

"WE WERE ATTACKED BY OUR OWN IRISH PEOPLE! WHY?"

"THE ENGLISH HAVE PUT A PRICE ON DONAL'S HEAD. FIVE HUNDRED GOLD DUCATS. A FORTUNE."

THE FOLLOWING DAY THEY WERE ATTACKED BY THE ENGLISH.

AND IN THE DAYS THAT FOLLOWED DONAL CAM'S FOLLOWERS WERE ATTACKED BY IRISH ANXIOUS FOR THE REWARD ALMOST AS OFTEN AS BY THE ENGLISH. THE LOSSES WERE VERY HIGH.

AND THOSE WHO REMAINED PAID FOR THEIR COURAGE.

"WE'VE BEEN TRICKED. O'SULLIVAN'S NOT HERE."

"KILL THEM. KILL THEM ALL!"

OVER ONE HUNDRED PEOPLE WERE SLAUGHTERED IN THE WOOD WHICH BECAME KNOWN AS THE OAK WOOD OF BLOOD, DOIRE NA FOLA.

"THERE'S WOOD APLENTY FOR THE FRAME, BUT WE'VE NO HIDES TO STRETCH ACROSS IT."

"KILL ALL THE HORSES BUT MINE. FLAY THEM."

DONAL CAM ONLY WEPT ONCE ON THE MARCH.

NEWS OF O'SULLIVANS APPROACH TRAVELLED QUICKLY.

"DONAL CAM WILL BE HERE WITHIN THE DAY."

"FIVE HUNDRED GOLD PIECES FOR THE MAN OR MEN WHO TAKE O'SULLIVAN."

"WHY AREN'T WE HELPING HIM? HE'S IRISH, LIKE US. WHY ARE WE HELPING THE ENGLISH?"

"WE DON'T HAVE A CHOICE ANYMORE: STAND WITH O'SULLIVAN AND YOU WILL DIE. THIS WAY WE HAVE A CHANCE."

ONE OF O'SULLIVAN'S FOLLOWERS APPEARS

"WE NEED SUPPLIES. WE WILL PAY ..."

"SEE HOW EASY IT IS? THEY ARE COLD AND HUNGRY. WE CAN TAKE THEM."

"WE ARE IRISHMEN KILLING IRISHMEN."

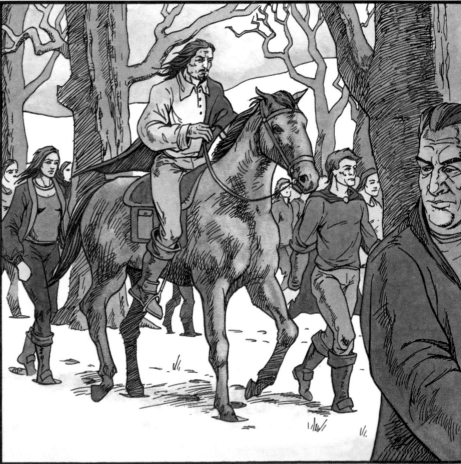

THE ATTACK IS BRIEF AND FURIOUS.

BUT O'SULLIVAN BEARE WAS NOT SO EASILY TAKEN.

"YOU BROUGHT THIS ON YOURSELF. IRISHMEN SHOULD NOT BE FIGHTING IRISHMEN!"

A MOAN.

"WHAT HAPPENED? AM I DEAD?"

"YOU'RE NOT DEAD. AND I WON'T LET YOU DIE."

"I'VE HEARD NEWS."

"IT'S OVER. O'SULLIVAN HAS REACHED LEITRIM. BUT O'NEILL HAD ALREADY SURRENDERED."

"NO, NOT FOR NOTHING. I FOUND YOU."

"THEN IT WAS ALL FOR NOTHING."

"HOW MANY MADE IT TO LEITRIM? A THOUSAND SET OUT..."

"THIRTY SIX."

CHAPTER SEVEN
NITS MAKE LICE: CROMWELL

INTRODUCTION

No name in Irish history is more hated than that of Oliver Cromwell. Appointed Lord Protector of Ireland by the English Parliament, Cromwell firmly believed the Irish to be idolatrous and barbarous savages, less than human. Besides, they were occupying fertile land that had been promised to supporters of the Parliamentarians in England's recent Civil War. The obvious solution was to exterminate them or, failing that, drive them to the very fringes of the island, to stony barren Connaught on the west coast.

Arriving in Ireland in 1649 with thirty five ships, Cromwell and his soldiers were accompanied by Puritan preachers obsessed with hatred for the Catholic Irish. From the pulpit they exhorted the invading army to "kill all that were, young men and old, children and maidens."

Cromwell's campaign opened at the city of Drogheda, which he determined to make an example that would terrify the rest of Ireland into submission. According to an officer in Cromwell's army, whose brother later became an historian at Oxford, the slaughter was tremendous. Some of the Cromwellians reputedly used Irish children as bucklers to protect themselves from the weapons the citizens of Drogheda snatched up in their own defence.

No one was to be spared, neither the Irish nor the 'Old English', earlier settlers and descendants of the Anglo-Normans who had by that time become 'more Irish than the Irish themselves'. The Drogheda garrison of three thousand was put to the sword. Meanwhile the civilian citizens of the town were also being slaughtered. Some apologists claim Cromwell did not actually order a massacre, but the infamous comment, "Nits make lice," used to justify the murder of infants, speaks for itself.

At the height of the horror his soldiers barricaded the doors of St. Peter's Church, where a number of terrified men, women and children had taken refuge in the steeple. Using the wooden pews for fuel, Cromwell's men set fire to the church. The hapless Catholics trapped inside were deliberately burned alive.

When news of Drogheda reached England, a day of public thanksgiving was proclaimed on 30 October.

After Drogheda was reduced to ashes and blood, Cromwell marched south to unleash a similar fury on Wexford. His army then swept across Ireland like a plague, battering castle and stronghold with their cannon, reducing towns to rubble. When he returned to England after nine months of the most savage destruction Ireland had ever seen, he was hailed as a hero. In his report to Parliament, Cromwell claimed, "This is a righteous judgement of God upon these barbarous wretches".

DROGHEDA, 10TH SEPTEMBER 1649.

THE CROMWELLIAN FORCES HAD BEEN BESIEGING THE TOWN SINCE EARLY SEPTEMBER.

THE ARMY WAS UNDER THE COMMAND OF OLIVER CROMWELL, LORD PROTECTOR OF IRELAND.

"NEWS FROM DROGHEDA. ASTON HAS REFUSED TO SURRENDER HIS GARRISON."

"I THOUGHT HE WOULD. ARROGANT FOOL. I HAVE PRAYED FOR GUIDANCE."

"I WAS LUCKY. YOUNG THOMAS AND RICHARD, THE BREWER'S SON, WERE NOT SO LUCKY."

"I HAVE PACKED A FEW THINGS. LET US GO NOW."

"THE HARBOUR IS BLOCKADED. WE ARE TRAPPED."

GUNS ROARED THROUGH THE NIGHT.

"WE WILL DIE TOMORROW."

"PROBABLY."

"IF WE SURVIVE THE MORROW, WE SHALL GO TO THE CHURCH OF SAINT PETER TO ASK GOD TO SPARE US YET ANOTHER DAY."

SEPTEMBER 11TH, THE FINAL ASSAULT.

THE FIGHTING WAS INTENSE, WITH NO QUARTER ASKED AND NONE GIVEN.

THERE WAS NOTHING TO DO BUT PRAY.

"AND THE PSALM SAITH, 'HAPPY SHALL HE BE THAT TAKETH AND DASHETH THY CHILDREN AGAINST THE STORM'."

WHEN THE WALLS WERE FINALLY BREACHED ASTON LED HIS GARRISON IN RETREAT.

BUT CROMWELL LED A CHARMED LIFE.

CROMWELL'S MEN DO NOT MISS.

"KILL THEM ALL!"

"GET HIS LEG! I HAVE HEARD THERE IS A FORTUNE IN GOLD COIN IN IT."

"IT IS EMPTY."

SIR ARTHUR ASTON WAS BEATEN TO DEATH WITH HIS WOODEN LEG. NONE OF HIS GARRISON WERE SPARED.

SAINT PETER'S CHURCH.

"WE ARE SAFE NOW."

BUT NO ONE WAS SAFE FROM THE BLOOD LUST NOW LOOSE IN THE STREETS OF DROGHEDA.

THOSE IN THE CHURCH RETREATED TO THE STEEPLE.

"SURRENDER NOW ... OR DIE."

THE DOORS WERE BOLTED.

CROMWELL'S MEN BROKE UP THE PEWS.

"FIRE!"

THERE WAS NO ESCAPE.

CHAPTER EIGHT

ORANGE AND GREEN: THE BATTLE OF THE BOYNE

INTRODUCTION

Following Cromwell's successful displacement of thousands of native Irish, a wave of 'plantation' took place. Settlers loyal to Protestantism were encouraged to take up land in Ireland. An influx of 'new' English and Scots repopulated Ulster. When the monarchy was restored in England, Charles II was well-disposed toward the Catholic Irish, and the Catholic 'Old English' as well. After his death, the crowns of England and Scotland passed to his brother James, an enthusiastic convert to Catholicism.

However, within four years James had so alienated the Parliament that he had to flee to France, where he sought the protection of his cousin Louis XIV. He was replaced on the throne by his Protestant daughter Mary and her husband, William, Prince of Orange. The French king, hoping to weaken his English rival William, encouraged James to make a bid to regain his kingdom and offered to supply him with troops.

1690 was a year of crisis. Two kings, James and William, were contesting for three kingdoms. Louis XIV of France was backing James II, the deposed Catholic king of England, against William III, a Protestant. The decisive battle between Jacobite and Williamite would be fought not on English soil however, but in Ireland. On the 1st. of July the Cromwellian landowners confronted the native Irish and the Old English Catholics on the banks of the Boyne River.

Those on the Jacobite side were fighting to regain the lands they had lost; the Williamites wanted to maintain a way of life that had already become well established. Continental troops swelled the ranks on both sides, reflecting European interests.

But ultimately it was the people of Ireland who would pay the price of victory – or defeat.

DAWN, JULY 1ST, 1690. THE VALLEY OF THE BOYNE RIVER.

SHE HEARS THE SOUND OF AN APPROACHING ARMY.

COUNT SCHOMBERG AT THE HEAD OF A WILLIAMITE DIVISION OF TEN THOUSAND MEN APPROACHES SLANE.

THE ARMY FOLLOWED THE BOYNE RIVER, PAST THE ANCIENT MOUND OF NEWGRANGE.

HERE THEY ENCOUNTERED SIR NEIL O'NEILL'S DRAGOONS, LOYAL TO JAMES.

THEIR ENCOUNTER WAS BRIEF AND BLOODY.

FOUR HUNDRED AND EIGHTY MEN FACING TEN THOUSAND.

THIS HAD ONCE BEEN A SACRED PLACE ... A HOLY PLACE...

"HELP ME."

ONE OF THE SOLDIERS WAS NOT DEAD.

"WATER."

AS SHE KNELT SHE REALISED SHE DIDN'T KNOW WHAT SIDE HE WAS FIGHTING ON.

"WHERE AM I?"

"NEAR NEWGRANGE."

"WHAT IS NEWGRANGE?"

"THE OLDEST, MOST SACRED SITE IN ALL IRELAND. A MAGIC PLACE."

KING WILLIAM OF ORANGE.

"JAMES IS LEAVING THE FIELD, SIRE. WE HAVE WON."

"WHY WERE YOU HERE?"

"I AM A SOLDIER."

"WHAT ARE YOU FIGHTING FOR?"

"I DON'T KNOW."

"WHAT ELSE CAN I DO?"

"YOU COULD FARM, THE EARTH IS RICH HERE."

"WHAT SIDE WERE YOU ON?"

"IT DOESN'T MATTER."

CHAPTER NINE

WHO FEARS TO SPEAK OF '98?

INTRODUCTION

In the years following the Battle of the Boyne, Ireland changed dramatically. Most of the Gaelic aristocracy had fled the country after Kinsale. Those who remained, together with the 'Old English', survived by submitting to the English crown and converting to Protestantism, thus joining the ruling class. They became known as the Anglo-Irish Ascendancy.

Theoretically, Ireland was a separate kingdom sharing a monarch with England. In actuality, it was a colony subjugated by its larger and more powerful neighbour. The peasantry learned the real meaning of colonialism. Under the Statutes of Kilkenny, the Irish language was outlawed. An education was denied the native Irish. Irish history was dismissed as myth and their religion as superstition. An ancient and highly artistic culture was all but destroyed, and Catholics became tenant farmers on land their ancestors had possessed for two thousand years.

The last half of the eighteenth century ushered in a new spirit of republicanism. In 1776 the Americans won their War of Independence; the French Revolution began in 1789. Encouraged by the fresh wind blowing elsewhere, political dissension in Ireland was building toward a crisis. Agrarian reforms were demanded; sectarian unrest was growing. While the oppressed suffered throughout the island, the elite enjoyed lives of stylish luxury. English law was the law of the land. Real power lay not with the Irish Parliament – although that body had been granted formal 'independence' in 1782 – but with the colonial administration in Dublin Castle, which was controlled by London.

Born in Dublin to a middle class family of comfortable circumstances, Theobald Wolfe Tone was a Protestant – yet he is recognised as being the first strong voice of Irish nationalism. A passionate visionary, Tone was incensed that the Irish Parliament failed to represent three quarters of Ireland, for Catholics could neither sit in it nor vote for its members.

He saw a breaking of the connection with England as the only cure for Ireland's social and economic ills. Toward that end Tone helped found the Society of United Irishmen, which included both Catholic and Protestant members.

In 1798 a series of uprisings broke out, primarily in Leinster. There was vicious fighting in Dublin; a company of insurgents was defeated at Tara, the ancient seat of kings. Protestant United Irishmen rose briefly in the Ulster counties of Down and Antrim, and in August 1798 became 'The Year of the French', when General Humbert landed in Co. Mayo with three shiploads of troops from France to aid the Irish cause. After some initial success they were soundly defeated. A second French contingent attempted a landing in Donegal in October, but was intercepted. Wolfe Tone was captured among them wearing the uniform of a French officer, and brought to Dublin to be tried for treason.

Condemned to hang, he attempted suicide, and died of a self-inflicted wound on the 19th of November.

By the time of Tone's death, approximately 30,000 had died in bloody rebellion. Ireland was punished for her attempt at revolution. Whole families were burned alive in their homes; wounded men were incinerated in a hospital at Enniscorthy. In reaction to the Rising of 1798, the Irish Parliament eventually voted for its own dissolution. In 1800, the Act of Union was passed by the British Parliament. When it came into effect on 1 January, 1801, Ireland officially became part of the United Kingdom.

1798 would be remembered, and the passions it kindled would survive to blaze in other men and women.

THE 18TH SEPTEMBER, 1803, ROBERT EMMET, SON OF A DUBLIN PHYSICIAN, WRITES HIS SWEETHEART FROM PRISON.

"MY DEAREST SARAH..."

"...MY BRIGHT LOVE."

"SARAH, WE CAME SO CLOSE ... WHAT A TIME IT WAS! OUR REBELLION REALLY BEGAN IN 1798 ...

...THE YEAR HUMBERT LANDED IN KILLALA BAY."

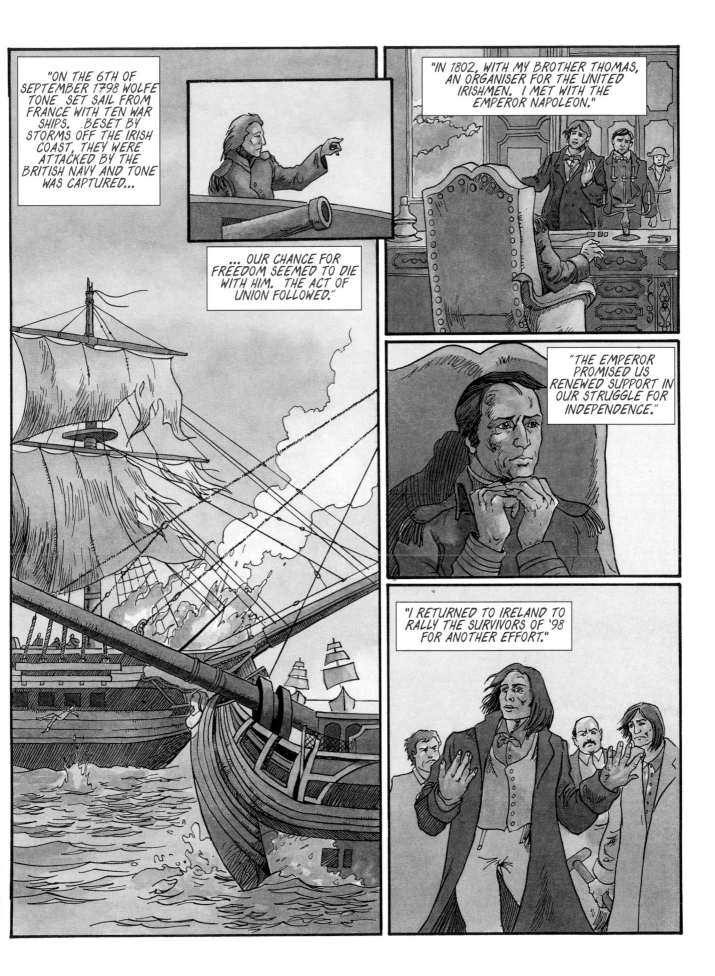

"ON THE 6TH OF SEPTEMBER 1798 WOLFE TONE SET SAIL FROM FRANCE WITH TEN WAR SHIPS. BESET BY STORMS OFF THE IRISH COAST, THEY WERE ATTACKED BY THE BRITISH NAVY AND TONE WAS CAPTURED...

...OUR CHANCE FOR FREEDOM SEEMED TO DIE WITH HIM. THE ACT OF UNION FOLLOWED."

"IN 1802, WITH MY BROTHER THOMAS, AN ORGANISER FOR THE UNITED IRISHMEN. I MET WITH THE EMPEROR NAPOLEON."

"THE EMPEROR PROMISED US RENEWED SUPPORT IN OUR STRUGGLE FOR INDEPENDENCE."

"I RETURNED TO IRELAND TO RALLY THE SURVIVORS OF '98 FOR ANOTHER EFFORT."

"BUT A MAN I TRUSTED PROVED TO BE A PAID SPY FOR DUBLIN CASTLE."

"I WAS BETRAYED."

"I WAS ON MY WAY TO YOU, MY SARAH."

ROBERT EMMET WAS PUBLICLY HANGED AND DECAPITATED ON THE 20TH SEPTEMBER, 1803.

BUT HIS WORDS LIVE ON: "LET NO MAN WRITE MY EPITAPH ... UNTIL MY COUNTRY TAKES HER PLACE AMONG THE NATIONS OF THE EARTH."

CHAPTER TEN

FAMINE: THE HUNGRY YEARS

INTRODUCTION

Nineteenth century Ireland was a pawn in the hands of various political forces. The Kerry-born lawyer and statesman Daniel O'Connell launched an unsuccessful campaign to repeal the Act of Union, but he did force the British government to concede Catholic Emancipation. The violence of the seventeenth and eighteenth centuries, however, had created an increasingly dangerous polarisation between Ireland's Catholics and Protestants.

Meanwhile, on an island whose population swelled in forty years from four million to eight million, the impoverished peasants were finding it increasingly difficult to survive. Once the natural resources of Ireland had supported her people bountifully. Now vast estates belonging to the landed gentry produced quantities of foodstuffs for the English market, while the Irish tenants who farmed them were allotted only tiny patches of the poorest land for their own subsistence. Upon these pitiful acres they grew potatoes.

The potato had been introduced into the country from the New World in the Elizabethan era, and the government deemed this an adequate diet for the Irish peasantry. For one third of the population it became the sole article of diet. Any other crops must be used to pay the rent. The cattle and corn they raised belonged to their landlords, they had no right to them, any more than they did to the deer in the forests or the fish in the rivers. The riches of Ireland were no longer theirs.

Edible though it might be, the potato had one serious drawback. A single variety had been introduced into Ireland, which meant no hybridisation took place. As the years passed the potato became weaker and more susceptible to disease. Crop failures increased. Then one morning in 1846 the Irish awoke to find their potatoes attacked by a devastating blight surpassing anything that had gone before. Within hours, fields of abundant green leaves turned into mires of rotting slime.

The potato blight raced like wildfire across Ireland. Some landlords tried to help their tenants, organising soup kitchens and even impoverishing themselves in order to aid the less fortunate. Other landlords, however, used the tenants' inability to pay rent as an excuse to pull down their homes around them and drive them from the land. The Irish starved in their own fields, their mouths green with the grass they tried to eat in their agony. By 1849 the death toll was estimated at anywhere from one to two million and nearly another million had emigrated to avoid starving.

AUGUST, 1849.

WITH THE POTATOES ROTTING IN THE GROUND THERE WAS NO HOPE FOR THEM ANYMORE...

...SHE CAN TELL BY THE SET OF HIS SHOULDERS WHAT HER HUSBAND HAS FOUND IN THE GROUND.

THERE IS SO LITTLE LEFT NOW...

...SO VERY LITTLE.

"FOR WHAT WE ARE ABOUT TO RECEIVE..."

"I DON'T LIKE THIS."

"I'M STILL HUNGRY."

"THERE IS NOTHING ELSE TO EAT."

"I'VE HEARD IT'S BAD EVERYWHERE. HUNDREDS, MAYBE THOUSANDS HAVE ALREADY DIED. THE COUNTRSIDE IS EMPTYING AS PEOPLE FLEE TO THE CITIES."

"BUT WHY, JACK? THERE'S NOTHING FOR THEM THERE."

"THERE'S SOUP AND BREAD."

"IF THEY'RE WILLING TO GIVE UP THEIR RELIGION AND SWEAR ALLEGIANCE TO THE PROTESTANT FAITH."

"AND IF THEY DON'T?"

"THEY DON'T EAT. I'VE HEARD THERE'S SICKNESS IN THE CITIES TOO. AND SO MANY DYING THERE'S NOT ENOUGH LEFT TO BURY THEM."

"WHAT ARE WE GOING TO DO, JACK? WHAT ABOUT THE CHILDREN?"

"WE CAN'T STAY HERE."

"WHERE WILL WE GO?"

"TO AMERICA!"

A HOME IN THE LAND OF OPPORTUNITY

PASSAGE TO AMERICA

GREATLY REDUCED ONE-WAY RATES

GENERATIONS HAD LIVED AND THRIVED ON THE LAND...

...NOW THERE WAS NOTHING TO KEEP THEM THERE ANYMORE.

"WHERE ARE YOU TAKING THEM?"

"THESE ARE THE PROPERTY OF HIS LORDSHIP. THEY'RE BEING SHIPPED TO LONDON FOR SLAUGHTER."

"ONE OF THOSE WOULD FEED US FOR A MONTH."

"TWO MONTHS."

THE OLD AND THE CHILDREN WERE ALWAYS THE FIRST TO DIE.

"MAY GOD HAVE MERCY ON THE SOUL OF THIS INNOCENT..."

"A SHIP'S IN. IT'S TAKING PASSENGERS FOR AMERICA."

"THERE'S NOTHING TO HOLD US HERE NOW."

UNSCRUPULOUS CAPTAINS WERE PREPARED TO CARRY PEOPLE IN SHIPS NOT FIT FOR ANIMALS.

DESPERATE PEOPLE WERE PREPARED TO ACCEPT THE CONDITIONS.

"WE SAIL IN TWO DAYS TIME. BE HERE, OR WE'LL GO WITHOUT YOU."

"WE'LL BE HERE."

"I HAD A DREAM, A NIGHTMARE."

"IT WAS ONLY A DREAM ... NOT ENOUGH FOOD."

"WE'LL DIE IF WE STAY."

"I DON'T WANT TO GO! WE'LL DIE IF WE GO."

"BUT AT LEAST WE'LL DIE IN IRELAND ... PERHAPS... IF GOD HAS MERCY ... WE MIGHT EVEN LIVE."

COFFIN SHIPS WERE LEAKY VESSELS UNFIT FOR SERVICE, DESPERATELY OVERCROWDED, UNDERSTOCKED WITH WATER AND FOOD. PEOPLE FRANTIC TO ESCAPE THE FAMINE PAID ALL THE MONEY THEY HAD FOR PASSAGE ON THESE VESSELS. THOUSANDS DIED EN ROUTE OF HUNGER AND DISEASE.

MANY OF THE SHIPS NEVER REACHED THEIR DESTINATION.

CHAPTER ELEVEN

THE UNCROWNED KING

INTRODUCTION

The Famine left Ireland exhausted and depopulated. Emigrants had fled their homeland in the hundreds of thousands, creating a tide that would never be reversed. The west, in particular, was studded with collapsing cottages that provided a mute testimonial to the curse of emigration.

In the 1870s, a campaign seeking Home Rule for Ireland began to gather strength. But it was not until the emergence of a leader in the form of Charles Stewart Parnell – a Protestant from a landlord family in County Wicklow – that the movement acquired a powerful voice. Throughout his life, Parnell would be an enigma. Seemingly a cold and remote man, he threw himself into politics with singleminded dedication, and later became involved in a passionate love affair that was the scandal of Ireland.

But there is no denying his successes. Upon being elected to the British House of Commons in 1875, he became an unyielding advocate for Ireland. He transformed the Home Rulers into the Irish Parliamentary Party, uniting a number of disparate political elements into a cohesive unit. Together with Michael Davitt, in 1879 he was involved in the founding of the National Land League which led to the first Land Act in 1881, a compromise measure that at least recognised a tenant's interest in his holding under certain conditions. By 1903, the latest version of the Land Act would see the transfer of huge tracts from the ownership of landlords to that of the common people.

Parnell and Davitt thus brought an end to the ancient evil of 'landlordism', under which a tenant's rent could be raised for no reason, or the women of his family abused, or his family evicted and their cabin pulled down to keep them from returning. The land issue had been a festering sore in Ireland for centuries. But success was not easily won. Michael Davitt was imprisoned for his activities on behalf of the movement.

The British Parliament was dominated by such personalities as Gladstone and Disraeli, both of whom used the 'Irish question' as a tool in electioneering. Parnell made himself increasingly unpopular with some by denouncing the policies of the government in Parliament, but nothing, not even imprisonment, could silence him. In 1886, Gladstone yielded to pressure and introduced a Home Rule bill. It was defeated, but the issue was now part of Parliament's agenda and would arise again.

Ulster responded to the threat to the Union – which had been so profitable for northern Protestants – by strengthening its own elected representation in Parliament. But a far different force was to destroy Parnell's power and the opportunities he was creating for Ireland. In 1890, Capt. William O'Shea sued his wife Katharine for divorce and named Parnell as co-respondent. The two had been devoted lovers for many years, maintaining what amounted to a marriage in all but name with the silent compliance of O'Shea, who profited from Parnell's support of him politically. But the public divorce suit resulted in a scathing denunciation of Parnell by the Catholic hierarchy in Ireland.

Following the divorce, Parnell promptly married Katharine. But it was too late. The party and nation he had so ably championed turned their back on him. His health, never robust, failed, and at the age of 45 he died in the arms of the woman he loved.

DECEMBER 24TH 1879.

CHRISTMAS TIME...

A TIME OF MERRIMENT...

... A TIME OF SECRETS.

"DAMN FINE SPEECH PARNELL MADE."

"ARROGANCE. THE MAN'S A TROUBLEMAKER. LAND FOR THE PEOPLE INDEED; WHOEVER HEARD THE LIKE?"

"GENTLEMEN, NO POLITICS, PLEASE! IT'S CHRISTMAS. A TIME OF GOOD CHEER."

BUT CHRISTMAS WAS NOT A TIME OF GOOD CHEER FOR EVERYONE.

HIS LORDSHIP'S SON.

"I HAVE SOMETHING TO TELL YOU."

"I'M GOING TO HAVE A CHILD."

"YOU SAID WE WOULD ELOPE."

"YOU PROMISED."

"AFTER CHRISTMAS. WE MUST NOT UPSET MY FATHER NOW."

CHRISTMAS DAY.

MANY IRISH PEASANTS LIVED IN POVERTY.

"AND HOW IS MY BABY SISTER?"

"HUNGRY! COLD!"

"LOOK WHAT I'VE BROUGHT. THE VERY BEST FROM HIS LORDSHIP'S KITCHENS."

"HAPPY CHRISTMAS."

"AND THIS IS FOR YOU, FATHER."

"WILL THEY NOT MISS IT UP AT THE HOUSE?"

"THERE'S SO MUCH THERE, FATHER, THEY'LL NEVER MISS IT."

"THE RENT HAS BEEN RAISED AGAIN."

"WHY?"

"THE ROOM FOR YOU AND YOUR SISTERS. HIS LORDSHIP'S BAILIFF SAID IT INCREASES THE VALUE OF THE PROPERTY, SO THEY'VE INCREASED THE RENT."

WE CAN'T AFFORD TO PAY IT."

"I HEARD TALK AT THE PARTY LAST NIGHT THAT MR PARNELL WANTS TO GIVE LAND TO THE PEOPLE."

"IT WILL NEVER HAPPEN."

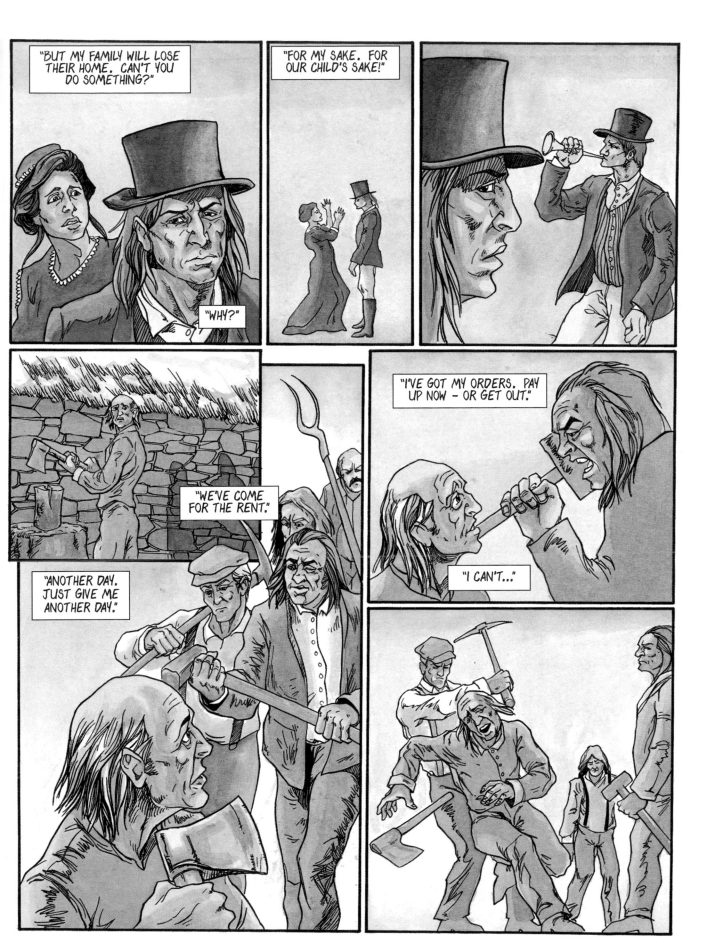

THE HUNTED....

...AND THE HUNTERS.

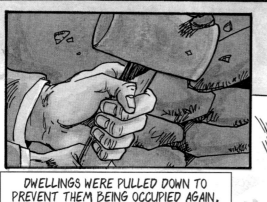
DWELLINGS WERE PULLED DOWN TO PREVENT THEM BEING OCCUPIED AGAIN.

"HELP US – PLEASE!"

"YOU SHOULD HAVE PAID YOUR RENT."

CHAPTER TWELVE

THE 1916 RISING

INTRODUCTION

In the aftermath of the Famine, Irish people began to dream of having their land back again, of being able to farm their own fields and keep their own crops. Long-smouldering hatred of foreign dominance erupted in sporadic violence.

New leaders arose in Ireland to challenge the power of the British establishment. Societies such as the Irish Republican Brotherhood and the Fenian Brotherhood encouraged nationalistic ideals. The Land League was founded to force agrarian reform, concentrating on landlords who were notorious for their mistreatment of tenants. But the triumphs of the Land League were not enough to satisfy the growing voices in Ireland that demanded real change.

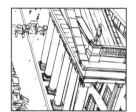

A Home Rule bill intended to give limited self-government to Ireland was introduced in Parliament early in the Twentieth century. Before it could be passed, organised opposition developed among the Protestants of Ulster, descendents of the earlier Cromwell plantations. As it had been for a thousand years the struggle was over the land, but this basic fact was disguised as a religious issue.

Claiming that Home Rule would mean Rome Rule, Ulster leaders actually began drilling soldiers in preparation for Civil War if Home Rule was granted. In response, the British government amended the bill to allow six counties of Ulster to opt out if they chose, at least for an initial period. This would mean partition of the island, which the majority of Irish people did not want. Volunteers in the south promptly emulated the Ulster Volunteers and began organising a resistance movement with the aim of gaining freedom from foreign rule for the entire island.

The outbreak of World War I saw thousands of Irish soldiers recruited into the British army to fight and die for a land not theirs. Meanwhile, the leaders of the Irish Volunteers began planning in earnest for revolution, taking advantage of the fact that England was occupied with war in Europe.

The Easter Rising began with Padraic Pearse, Commander-in-Chief of the Irish Volunteers, standing on the steps of the General Post Office in Dublin and reading a proclamation declaring "the right of the people of Ireland to the ownership of Ireland".

War for independence had been declared.

The following week would see much of Dublin reduced to rubble. Badly organised and betrayed by a breakdown in communications and support, the rebels fought valiantly but finally surrendered to prevent further bloodshed.

DUBLIN, EASTER SUNDAY, 1916.

IN THE HEART OF THE WEALTHY CITY EXIST SOME OF THE WORST SLUMS IN EUROPE.

"OWING TO THE VERY CRITICAL POSITION, ALL ORDERS GIVEN TO IRISH VOLUNTEERS FOR EASTER SUNDAY ARE HEREBY RESCINDED AND NO PARADES, MARCHES OR OTHER MOVEMENTS OF IRISH VOLUNTEERS WILL TAKE PLACE."

"THE MARCH IS CANCELLED. WHY?"

"A MISUNDERSTANDING."

"MARCHES WILL GO AHEAD TOMORROW AS PLANNED."

THE SLUMS OF DUBLIN HAD ONE OF THE HIGHEST INCIDENCES OF TUBERCULOSIS IN THE WORLD, CLAIMING OVER 1,000 VICTIMS A YEAR.

"I HEARD THE DOOR. WHAT'S THE NEWS?"

"TOMMY SAYS THE MARCHES WILL GO AHEAD TOMORROW."

"PLEASE DON'T GO. I HAD A DREAM ... A TERRIBLE DREAM."

"NOTHING WILL HAPPEN. IT'S JUST ANOTHER MARCH."

"NOT THIS TIME."

"TELL HIM."

"HE WON'T LISTEN."

"WEAR THESE; MY PRAYERS GO WITH THEM."

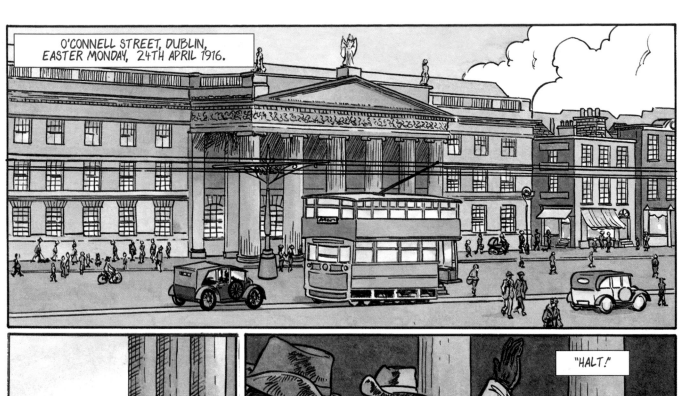

O'CONNELL STREET, DUBLIN, EASTER MONDAY, 24TH APRIL 1916.

"HALT!"

AT 12 NOON, THE REBELS STORMED THE GENERAL POST OFFICE.

"THE GPO ... CHARGE!"

IT TOOK ONLY MINUTES TO SECURE THE BUILDING...

THE GREAT ADVENTURE HAD BEGUN.

MOST ONLOOKERS WERE ASTONISHED BY EVENTS.

BRITISH LANCERS ON A ROUTINE MISSON HAVE HEARD RUMOURS OF TROUBLE IN SACKVILLE STREET.

"DON'T FIRE, DON'T FIRE UNTIL I GIVE THE WORD. PASS IT ON."

"DON'T FIRE ... DON'T FIRE..."

"REBELS HAVE TAKEN THE GPO."

"CHARGE!"

A SHOT RINGS OUT.

THINKING THE SIGNAL HAS BEEN GIVEN, MEN FIRE A VOLLEY OF SHOTS.

ANOTHER VOLLEY RINGS OUT.

THE FIRST SHOTS OF THE RISING HAD BEEN FIRED,
THE FIRST CASUALTIES SUFFERED.

DUBLINERS ARE
TAKEN BY SURPRISE.

THEIR SURPRISE TURNS TO ANGER.

"SHAME!"

A BOY DARTS OUT
OF THE CROWD.

"GET BACK HERE, YOU!"

"I WANT TO JOIN THEM."

"NO, YOU'RE NOT!"

AS THE AFTERNOON WORE ON, MEN CREPT OUT FROM THE GPO TO GATHER SUPPLIES FROM THE SURROUNDING SHOPS.

IN EVERY CASE THEY LEFT RECEIPTS.

"SEAN!"

"COME HOME. MAMA WANTS YOU."

"I CAN'T, I'M NEEDED HERE."

LATER STILL THE ORDINARY PEOPLE OF DUBLIN GREW INCREASINGLY AGITATED WITH THE INSURRECTIONISTS.

"WE'VE COME TO COLLECT OUR BRITISH ARMY SEPARATIONS ALLOWANCE."

"ALL ALLOWANCES HAVE CEASED. WE'RE IN CONTROL NOW,"

SEAN HAD NOT QUITE REALISED THE CONTEMPT THE ORDINARY PEOPLE OF DUBLIN HAD FOR THE INSURRECTIONISTS.

"AND WHAT HAPPENED THEN?"

"BARRICADES WERE ERECTED AROUND THE GPO, CLOSING OFF THE STREETS."

"AND THEN, LATER IN THE AFTERNOON, PEOPLE STARTED LOOTING THE SHOPS."

"AND WHERE WERE THE POLICE?"

"THERE WERE NO POLICE ON THE STREETS."

"MR. PEARSE SENT OUT SOME MEN TO CHASE THE PEOPLE AWAY."

"AND SEAN, WHAT OF SEAN?"

TUESDAY WAS RELATIVELY QUIET, WITH BOTH SIDES CONSOLIDATING THEIR POSITIONS, BUT ON WEDNESDAY MORNING...

"CANNONS!"

"IT HAS TO END SOON NOW."

THE PEOPLE OF DUBLIN HAD NOT SUPPORTED THE RISING. WITHOUT THEIR SUPPORT THE REVOLUTION COULD NOT POSSIBLY SUCCEED.

IT WAS ALMOST OVER NOW, HE KNEW THAT.

TOGETHER WITH OTHER LEADERS OF THE RISING, THE SIGNATORIES OF THE EASTER PROCLAMATION WERE PROMPTLY EXECUTED BY THE BRITISH GOVERNMENT. THEY INCLUDED TOM CLARKE, A TOBACCONIST, SEAN MACDERMOTT, A FOUNDER OF THE IRB, PADRAIC PEARSE, A SCHOOLTEACHER, JAMES CONNOLLY, A LABOUR ORGANISER, EAMONN CEANNT, A SCHOOLTEACHER, THOMAS MACDONOGH, AN ACADEMIC, AND JOSEPH PLUNKETT, WHO WAS DYING OF TUBERCULOSIS. FIVE HAD WRITTEN BOOKS; FOUR WERE PUBLISHED POETS. WITHOUT EXCEPTION, THEY WENT BRAVELY TO THEIR DEATHS, BELIEVING THEIR EASTER RISING HAD FAILED. BUT THEIR EXECUTIONS HAD A PROFOUND AND LASTING EFFECT ON THE IRISH PEOPLE.

CHAPTER THIRTEEN
THE TROUBLES

INTRODUCTION

Within six years of the Easter Rising, the Irish, resolved to see that the sacrifice had not been in vain, achieved Free State status within the British Commonwealth. But the price was high – partition. Ireland was racked by Civil War between those supporting the Treaty with England and those opposed, who wanted to see all Ireland united as one nation.

Then on the 18th of April, 1949, twenty six of the island's thirty two counties formally left the Commonwealth to become the Republic of Ireland, sovereign and independent. Only six counties of Ulster, now known as Northern Ireland, remained part of the United Kingdom.

The divided island settled into an uneasy peace. The Republic was occupied with building a new nation from scratch, learning self-government, competing independently for the first time with more powerful, established nations. At first the economy was very bad; centuries of colonialism had all but stripped Ireland of her natural resources, while years of conflict had sapped the energy of the people.

Meanwhile Northern Ireland, supported by the United Kingdom, flourished by comparison. The existing sectarian divide was enlarged with Protestants loyal to the Crown finding employment while the Catholics who remained in the north after Partition found themselves the objects of massive economic and social discrimination. People who had lived amicably side by side for years were turned against each other by those who sought to exploit the situation. Religious antagonism was encouraged by hatemongers.

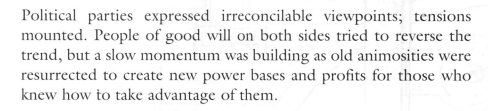

Political parties expressed irreconcilable viewpoints; tensions mounted. People of good will on both sides tried to reverse the trend, but a slow momentum was building as old animosities were resurrected to create new power bases and profits for those who knew how to take advantage of them.

Civil rights marches patterned on those in the United States were organised in Northern Ireland in the sixties, as the underprivileged fought for equality. On the 5th of October in 1968, a civil rights march in Derry – then known as Londonderry – erupted in violence. Eighty eight were injured, including eleven policemen. An escalating spiral of confrontation followed, climaxing in the day which would go down in Irish history as Bloody Sunday.

On January 30, 1972, members of a British parachute regiment killed fourteen unarmed civilians in Derry at an anti-internment demonstration. The people were protesting the policy of arrest without a specified crime, designed to take those perceived to be dangerous off the streets. But the real danger was on the streets that day, and the hatred born of Bloody Sunday would poison the decades to follow, filling the streets of Belfast and Derry with soldiers, turning quiet housing estates into armed camps, denying the most basic tenets of Christianity which both sides claimed to follow.

The Troubles had begun.

THE TIME OF DREAMING IS OVER.

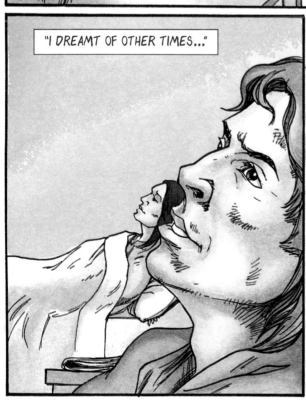

"I DREAMT OF OTHER TIMES..."

"SO DID I..."

Sources

Chapter 1: The Mystery of Newgrange

Brennan, Martin, THE BOYNE VALLEY VISION, The Dolmen Press, Dublin, 1980
Brennan, Martin, THE STARS AND THE STONES, Thames & Hudson, London, 1983
Herity, Michael, and Eogan, George, IRELAND IN PREHISTORY, Routledge & Kegan Paul, London, 1977
Herity, Michael, IRISH PASSAGE GRAVES, Irish University Press, Dublin, 1974
Martin, C. P., PREHISTORIC MAN IN IRELAND, Macmillan & Co., London, 1935
Movius, Hallam L. THE IRISH STONE AGE, Cambridge University Press, 1969
O'Kelly, Michael J., EARLY IRELAND, AN INTRODUCTION TO IRISH PREHISTORY, Cambridge University Press, 1989
O'Kelly, Michael J., NEWGRANGE, Thames & Hudson, London, 1982
O'Riordain, Sean, and Daniel, Glyn, NEW GRANGE, Thames & Hudson, London, 1964
Raftery, Joseph, PREHISTORIC IRELAND, B. T. Batsford, London, 1951

Chapter 2: The Fire on the Hill: St. Patrick

Dalton, E. A., HISTORY OF IRELAND, Vol. I, to the year 1210, The Gresham Publishing Co., Belfast, n.d.
D'Arcy, Mary Ryan, THE SAINTS OF IRELAND, The Irish American Cultural Institute, St.. Paul, Minnesota,1974
De Paor, Liam, SAINT PATRICK'S WORLD, Four Courts Press, Dublin, Ireland, 1993
Heron, James, THE CELTIC CHURCH IN IRELAND, Service & Paton, London, 1898
Joyce, Patrick Weston, HISTORY OF GAELIC IRELAND, Longmans, Green & Co., London, 1924
Kenney, James F., SOURCES FOR THE EARLY HISTORY OF IRELAND, THE, Columbia University Press, New York, 1929
Lehane, Brendan, EARLY CELTIC CHRISTIANITY, Constable, London, 1994
Reilly, Robert, IRISH SAINTS, Wings Books, New York, 1964
Scherman, Katharine, THE FLOWERING OF IRELAND, Little, Brown & Co., Boston, 1981
Thompson, E. A., WHO WAS SAINT PATRICK?, St. Martin's Press, New York, 1985

Chapter 3: Viking

Brent, Peter, THE VIKING SAGA, G.P. Putnam's Sons, New York, 1975
Brondsted, Johannes, THE VIKINGS, Pelican, Middlesex, 1965
Flood, J. M., THE NORTHMEN IN IRELAND, Browne & Nolan Ltd., Dublin, n.d.
Graham-Campbell, James, THE VIKING WORLD, Ticknor & Fields, New York, 1980
Jones, Gwyn, A HISTORY OF THE VIKINGS, Oxford University Press, London, 1968
La Fay, Howard, THE VIKINGS, National Geographic Society, Washington, D. C., 1972
Magnusson, Magnus, VIKINGS!, The Bodley Head, London, 1980
Sawyer, P. H., KINGS AND VIKINGS, Methuen & Co., London, 1982
Uppsala University, THE VIKING, AB Nordbok, Sweden, 1975
Wilson, David M., editor, THE NORTHERN WORLD, Harry Abrams, New York, 1980

Chapter 4: Brian Boru and the Battle at Clontarf

Clerigh, Arthur, THE HISTORY OF IRELAND TO THE COMING OF HENRY II, T. Fisher Unwin, London, n.d.

Curtis, Edmund, A HISTORY OF IRELAND, Methuen & Co., London, 1952

Green, Alice Stopford, HISTORY OF THE IRISH STATE TO 1014, Macmillan & Co., London, 1925

Joyce, Patrick Weston, HISTORY OF GAELIC IRELAND, Longmans, Green & Co. London, 1924

Mac Airt, Sean, translator, THE ANNALS OF INISFALLEN, Dublin Institute for Advanced Studies, Dublin, 1977

Newman, Roger Chatterton, BRIAN BORU, Anvil Books, Dublin, 1983

O'Brien, Donough, THE HISTORY OF THE O'BRIENS, B. T. Batsford, London, n.d.

O'Donovan, John, editor, ANNALS OF THE FOUR MASTERS, Vol. II, reprinted byDe Burca Rare Books, Dublin, 1990

Stokes, Whitley, translator, THE ANNALS OF TIGERNACH, VOL. II, Llanerch Publishers, Wales, 1993

Todd, James, translator, WAR OF THE GAEDHILL WITH THE GAILL, Longmans Green, London, 1867

Chapter 5: A Wedding in Waterford: Strongbow and Aoife

Barnard, Francis P., STRONGBOW'S CONQUEST OF IRELAND, G.P. Putnam's Sons, New York, 1888

Curtis, Edmund, A HISTORY OF MEDIEVAL IRELAND, Methuen & Co., London, 1978

D'Alton, E. A., HISTORY OF IRELAND, Vol. I, to the year 1210, The Gresham Publishing Co., Belfast, n.d.

Furlong, Nicholas, DERMOT, KING OF LEINSTER, Anvil Press, Dublin,1973

Hull, Eleanor, A HISTORY OF IRELAND AND HER PEOPLE, Vol. I, Phoenix Publishing Co. Dublin, n. d.

MacGearailt, Gearoid, CELTS AND NORMANS, Gill & Macmillan, Dublin, 1969

MacNeill, Eoin, PHASES OF IRISH HISTORY, Kennikat Press, New York, 1970

O'Corrain, Donncha, IRELAND BEFORE THE NORMANS, The Gill History of Ireland Series, Gill and Macmillan, Dublin, 1972

O'Donovan, John, editor, ANNALS OF THE FOUR MASTERS, Vol. II, reprinted by De Burca Rare Books, Dublin, 1990

Sheehy, Maurice, WHEN THE NORMANS CAME TO IRELAND, Mercier Press, Cork, 1975

Chapter 6: The Long March

Berleth, Richard, THE TWILIGHT LORDS, Alfred A. Knopf, New York,1978

Carew, Sir George, PACATA HIBERNIA, A HISTORY OF THE WARS IN IRELAND, Downey & Co., London, 1896

Mac Curtain, Margaret, TUDOR AND STUART IRELAND, The Gill History of Ireland series, Gill & Macmillan, Dublin, 1972

Moryson, Fynes, ITINERARY, John Beale, London, 1617

O'Donovan, John, editor, ANNALS OF THE FOUR MASTERS, Vol. VI, reprinted by De Burca Rare Books, Dublin, 1990

O'Faolain, Sean, THE GREAT O'NEILL, Longmans, Green, London, 1942

O'Siodhachain, Donal, THE GREAT RETREAT, Clo Duanaire, Cork, 1987

O'Sullivan, Don Philip, A HISTORY OF IRELAND IN THE REIGN OF ELIZABETH, translated by Matthew J. Byrne, Sealy Bryers & Walker, Dublin, 1903

Silke, John J., KINSALE, Fordham University Press, New York, 1970

Sullivan, T. D., BANTRY, BEREHAVEN, AND THE O'SULLIVAN SEPT, Sealy, Bryers, & Walker, Dublin, 1908

Chapter 7: Nits Make Lice: Cromwell

Bottigheimer, Karl S., IRELAND AND THE IRISH, Columbia University Press, New York, 1982

Canny, Nicholas, FROM REFORMATION TO RESTORATION, IRELAND 1534-1660, Helicon Ltd., Dublin, 1987

Clarke, Aidan, THE OLD ENGLISH IN IRELAND, 1625-42, Macgibbon & Kee, London, 1966

Curtis, Edmund, A HISTORY OF IRELAND, Methuen & Co., London, 1952

FitzGibbon, Constantine, THE IRISH IN IRELAND, W.W. Norton & Co., New York, 1983

Foster, R.F., MODERN IRELAND 1600 - 1972, Allen Lane, The Penguin Press, London, 1988

Fraser, Antonia, CROMWELL: OUR CHIEF OF MEN, Weidenfeld & Nicolson, London, 1973

Mac Curtain, Margaret, TUDOR AND STUART IRELAND, The Gill History of Ireland Series, Gill and Macmillan, Dublin, 1972

MacLysaght, Edward, IRISH LIFE IN THE SEVENTEENTH CENTURY, Longmans, Green & Co., London, 1939

Murphy, Denis, CROMWELL IN IRELAND, M. H. Gill & Son, Dublin, 1897

Chapter 8: Orange and Green: The Battle of the Boyne

Churchill, Winston, S. , A HISTORY OF THE ENGLISH SPEAKING PEOPLES, Vol. III, Dodd, Mead & Co., New York, 1965
Curtis, Edmund, A HISTORY OF IRELAND, Methuen & Co., London, 1952
D'Alton, E. A., HISTORY OF IRELAND, Vol. IV, The Gresham Publishing Co., Belfast, n.d.
Durant, Will and Ariel, THE AGE OF LOUIS XIV, Simon & Schuster, New York, 1963
Foster, R. F., MODERN IRELAND, 1600-1972, Allen Lane, The Penguin Press, London, 1988
Green, Howard, THE BATTLEFIELDS OF BRITAIN AND IRELAND, Constable, London, 1973
Hayes, G.A., Mc Coy, IRISH BATTLES, Gill and Macmillan, Dublin,1969
Hull, Eleanor, A HISTORY OF IRELAND, Vol. II, , Phoenix Publishing Co. Dublin, n.d.
Johnston, Edith Mary, IRELAND IN THE EIGHTEENTH CENTURY, The Gill History of Ireland Series, Gill and Macmillan, London, 1974
MacManus, Seamus, THE STORY OF THE IRISH RACE, Kevin-Adair, New York, 1966

Chapter 9: Who Fears to Speak of '98

Curtis, Edmund, A HISTORY OF IRELAND, Methuen & Co., London, 1952
Elliott, Marianne, WOLFE TONE, Yale University Press, 1989
FitzGibbon, Constantine, THE IRISH IN IRELAND, David & Charles, London, 1983
Furlong, Nicholas, FATHER JOHN MURPHY OF BOOLAVOGUE, 1753-1798, Geography Publications, Dublin 1991
Foster, R.F., MODERN IRELAND 1600-1972, Allen Lane, The Penguin Press, London, 1988
Magnusson, Magnus, LANDLORD OR TENANT, The Bodley head, London, 1978
Moley, Raymond. DANIEL O'CONNELL; NATIONALISM WITHOUT VIOLENCE, Fordham University Press, 1974
Neill, Kenneth, AN ILLUSTRATED HISTORY OF THE IRISH PEOPLE, Mayflower Books, New York, 1979
Tone, Wolfe, THE LIFE OF WOLFE TONE, The Educational Company of Ireland Ltd., n.d.

Chapter 10: Famine: The Hungry Years

De Breffny, Brian, editor, THE IRISH WORLD, Harry Abrams, New York, 1977
Fitzgibbon, Constantine, THE IRISH IN IRELAND, W. W. Norton & Co., New York, 1983
Foster, R. F., MODERN IRELAND 1600-1972, Allen Lane, The Penguin Press, London, 1988
Gallagher, Thomas, PADDY'S LAMENT, Harcourt Brace Jovanovich, New York, 1982
Hickey & Doherty, A DICTIONARY OF IRISH HISTORY SINCE 1800, Gill and Macmillan, Dublin, 1980
Hull, Eleanor, A HISTORY OF IRELAND, Vol. II, The Phoenix Publishing Company, Dublin, n.d.
Magnusson, Magnus, TENANT OR LANDLORD?, The Bodley Head, in association with BBC, London, 1978
Neill, Kenneth, AN ILLUSTRATED HISTORY OF THE IRISH PEOPLE, Mayflower Books, New York, 1979
Ranelagh, John, IRELAND, AN ILLUSTRATED HISTORY, Oxford University Press, New York, 1981
Scott, Michael, ed., HALL'S IRELAND, Mr & Mrs Samuel Carter Hall's Tour of Ireland 1840-1845, London, 1983
Woodham-Smith, Cecil, THE GREAT HUNGER, Hamish Hamilton, London, 1964

Chapter 11: The Uncrowned King

FitzGibbon, Constantine, THE IRISH IN IRELAND, David & Charles, London, 1983
Foster, R.F., MODERN IRELAND 1600-1972, Allen Lane, The Penguin Press, London, 1988
Foster, R.F., CHARLES STEWART PARNELL; THE MAN AND HIS FAMILY, Hassocks, London, 1976
Hull, Eleanor, A HISTORY OF IRELAND AND HER PEOPLE, Phoenix Publishing Co. Ltd., Dublin, n.d.
Kelly, John S., THE BODYKE EVICTIONS, Fossabeg Press, Co. Clare, 1987
Lee, Joseph, THE MODERNISATION OF IRISH SOCIETY, The Gill History of Ireland Series, Gill & MacMillan, 1973
Magnusson, MAgnus, LANDLORD OR TENANT, The Bodley Head, London, 1978

Chapter 12: The 1916 Rising

Connolly O'Brien, Nora, THE IRISH REBELLION OF 1916, New York, 1918
Edwards, Ruth Dudley, PATRICK PEARSE, THE TRIUMPH OF FAILURE, Taplinger Publishing Co., New York, 1978
McHugh, Roger, DUBLIN 1916, Arlington Books, London, 1976
Martin, F.X., editor, LEADERS AND MEN OF THE EASTER RISING, DUBLIN 1916, Methuen & Co., London, 1967
O'Brien, M. & C.C., A CONCISE HISTORY OF IRELAND, Beekman House, New York, 1972
O'Rahilly, Aodogan, WINDING THE CLOCK, O'RAHILLY AND THE 1916 RISING, The Lilliput Press, Dublin, 1991
Stephens, James, THE INSURRECTION IN DUBLIN, Maunsel & Co., Ltd., Dublin, 1916

Chapter 13: The Troubles

Foster, R. F., MODERN IRELAND 1600-1972, Allen Lane, The Penguin Press, London, 1988
Holland, Jack, TOO LONG A SACRIFICE, Dodd, Mead & Co. New York, 1981
Hopkinson, Michael, GREEN AGAINST GREEN, Gill & Macmillan, Dublin, 1988
Kiely, Benedict, COUNTIES OF CONTENTION, Mercier Press, Cork, 1945
Macardle, Dorothy, THE IRISH REPUBLIC, Victor Gollancz, London, 1951
McCann, Eamonn, BLOODY SUNDAY IN DERRY, Brandon Books, Kerry, 1992
O'Connor, Ulick, THE TROUBLES, Hamish Hamilton, London, 1975
O'Malley, Ernie, ON ANOTHER MAN'S WOUND, Dublin, 1936
O'Malley, Ernie, THE SINGING FLAME, Anvil Books, Dublin, 1978
Younger, Calton, IRELAND'S CIVIL WAR, Frederick Muller Ltd., London, 1968

ABOUT THIS BOOK

In the past, few learned much history from academic books. The vast majority of people around the world learned about the past through a collection of sometimes mythical tales which had been handed down from generation to generation.

Many of the problems experienced in Northern Ireland can be traced back to such folkloric history.

Stories about papist conspiracy and loyalist bigotry, although sometimes containing a seed of truth, have instilled deep and dangerous prejudices. If such stories are allowed to grow unchallenged, these prejudices may remain forever in spite of the best-intentioned peace initiatives. All the academic history books in the world will not change attitudes. Children and adults alike need to see, feel and live history to learn its lessons and grasp its meanings.

Few can take the time or have the inclination. In-depth visual storytelling overcomes this problem. In this way we bring back the bard and apply the bardic skills to the telling of history. It is not enough to know when Napoleon was defeated at Waterloo or when Cromwell stormed Drogheda to understand how such events have influenced our subconscious and can affect actions even today. We must go back and share the feelings of the people involved. We must take part in their lives.

IRELAND, A GRAPHIC HISTORY is not just another history. It is a pioneering effort to employ a new medium, the graphic novel, to carry us back in time, to allow us to feel the joy and sorrows of ordinary people experiencing extraordinary events.

An exceptional effort was required to produce such a book and make it work. Attempting to cover 6,000 years of Irish history in 176 pages is no easy feat. A great number of separate elements and people were necessary. Authors Morgan Llywelyn and Michael Scott brought extensive historical knowledge and undisputed storytelling abilities to the project and were perfectly equipped to take up the challenge. The publishers, Gill and Macmillan and Element Books, whose daring and enthusiasm have been invaluable, had the necessary experience to make the book a reality.

An army of artists under the guidance of Will Eisner pored over the drawings night and day. They had both appetite and stamina for such a project. They include: Eoin Coveney – the lead illustrator; David Smith – the lead inker; Laurence Herbert – the lead colourist; assisted by:

> Roger Horgan – inker/colourist; Vicki Jocher – colourist; Damian Foley – colourist; John Hussey – colourist; Darren Nesbitt – research; Mark Smullen, Oisin McGann, John Hussey – retouchers; David Duffy, Grainne O'Rourke – text layout and assembly; and Steve Simpson – cover designer (all members of Springboard, the Graphic Storytellers' Alliance).

The entire book was written, designed, and illustrated in Ireland, using artists from north and south of the border, working in close alliance with the master Will Eisner from the USA and with the British and Irish publishers in a model of international co-operation. It was not easy ... but everyone involved believed it was worth doing.

DUDLEY STEWART
DUBLIN, IRELAND